HTML

CASSELL&CO

First published in the United Kingdom in 2000 by Hachette UK
ISBN 1 84202 056 0

Designed by Chouka / Typeset in Sabon MT / Printed and bound in Germany

English translation by Prose Unlimited

Concept and editorial direction: Gheorghii Vladimirovitch Grigorieff

Additional editorial assistance: Andrew Bolton, Huw Jones

A CIP catalogue for this book is available from the British Library.

Hachette UK

Cassell & Co

The Orion Publishing Group

Wellington House

125 Strand

London

WC2R 0BB

© English Translation Hachette UK 2000

© Marabout 2000

TABLE OF CONTENTS

Introduction

INTRODUCTION

HTML (Hypertext Markup Language) is the program language used to write documents in hypertext that can be viewed on equipment connected to the World Wide Web (www or just the Web).

The document and the objects it comprises such as images, sounds, files, etc. are known as **resources**.

To translate an HTML document (e.g. a Web page) into something comprehensible to humans (text, images, sounds, etc.), the computer needs a *user agent*, which is usually a *Web browser* (or navigator). The best-known are Netscape Navigator and Microsoft Explorer, but others are available. The hardware can be any computer platform — Sun, PC, Mac, etc. — or even a mobile telephone or a television.

To display a Web page, a browser must know where to find it among the thousands of servers: it must know its *precise address* (URL, or Uniform Resource Locator) on the Internet.

The Internet is a mass memory, like an immense hard disk dispersed around the planet. When you log on to the Internet, you have access to all or part of this mass memory: most of the areas are public, but some are private and require access rights.

As on a hard disk, you must be able to locate the file you want to use. Whether it is an HTML page or an image or an audio file, you have to know the right *access path* to this file.

The Web page URL specifies the access path and the name of the resource. It is a character string that looks something like:

http://www.microsoft.com/index.html

If you type this line in the address field of your browser, it will display the page called index.html. This is the quickest way to access a Web page. When you define a page as a 'Favorite' or 'Startup page', the browser memorises its URL.

The URL specifies the type of server, symbolised by the acronym of the protocol it uses. For the Web it is **http://**. However, the Web is only a part of the Internet, a global network that includes domains that use protocols such as Telnet, Gopher, News, e-mail, etc. HTML enables links with these domains from a Web page read by a browser, which gives the user the impression that the Internet is a uniform whole.

1

How HTML works

How HTML works

To communicate **content** (text, images, sounds, animations, etc.) and **instructions** to the browser interpretation engine, HTML uses ASCII: an agreed standard set of alphanumeric characters and symbols. This makes it possible to write a Web page using a very basic text editor such as NotePad.

The instructions in the Web page explain to the browser what it must do with the contents: for example, display the text in boldface, underline it, precede it with a bullet, load a file, display an image, find another page, etc. HTML consists of over a hundred instructions (which define *elements*) that can be modified by properties (*attributes*). HTML relies on fewer than 200 keywords and uses a syntax which resembles natural English.

1. Elements and tags

In HTML, each instruction for the browser is embedded in the text content. The document's structure and appearance are dictated by these instructions, which identify elements such as headings, paragraphs, lists, graphics, tables or links to other Web pages.

An element comprises three parts: a **start instruction**, the **content** and an **end instruction**. The instructions are expressed as **tags**.

For example, the keyword I is used to display the text in italics. All HTML tags are enclosed in angle brackets (<>). The element **I** is made up of the following parts:

a start tag:
in this case, the **<I>** tag instructs the browser to display in italics the text that follows;

the content:
the resource (text, image, sound, file, etc.) affected by the start tag; the tag <I> can only be applied to

text (some elements are applicable only to certain types of resources);

an end tag:
this is the same as the start tag, except a forward slash (/) precedes the keyword. In this case, the tag `</I>` instructs the browser to stop displaying in italics the text that follows.

The code

```
<I>Hello world</I>Hello world.
```

would appear as

Hello world Hello world.

In practice, even in specialised documentation, the terms 'instruction', 'tag', 'element' and 'keyword' are used interchangeably. This is unlikely to lead to confusion, because it is very easy to distinguish tags (instructions) from content.

Distinguishing instructions from content

The browser reads a page sequentially, from beginning to end. It can distinguish an instruction from content (e.g., the text to display), because instructions are always enclosed in angle brackets. Any text placed between the brackets is interpreted as an instruction and will not be displayed: the browser will know it is an instruction, and that this instruction concerns what follows it.

The instruction **<B>** tells the browser: 'Display what follows in boldface.'

So if we have

    <B>Hello

the browser will display

Hello

Note

The browser will continue to display in boldface EVERYTHING that follows the tag <B>. To stop the bold action, you must give another instruction to the browser, including the end tag </B>.

We will therefore have:

<B>
which means: 'Start boldface', and

</B>
which means 'Stop boldface.'

So the text

The quick brown <B>fox</B> jumps over the lazy<B>dog</B>.

will be interpreted by the browser (and displayed) as follows:

The quick brown **fox** jumps over the lazy **dog**.

The end tags need not be memorised, since they are derived from the start tags: <B> and </B>, <I> and </I>, etc.

 Note that a tag does not replace a character space, for example between words or sentences.

```
Including comments that are
   not to be displayed
```

Instructions are not displayed verbatim by the browser, which treats everything enclosed in angle brackets as an instruction.

If the text enclosed in angle brackets is not a standard instruction, the browser considers it to be a wrong tag or one that belongs to an HTML version for which it is not equipped, and usually ignores its instructions.

The code

<Author: JP Lovinfosse>

will not be displayed, but could upset certain browsers, which will try to interpret this strange tag.

The author may nevertheless wish to include comments not intended for the reader but for him/herself or those who will update the document in future. In HTML, comments not intended for display must be enclosed in <!-- and --> tags, and the character string '--' cannot be used in the comment.

The code

<!-- Author: JP Lovinfosse -->

will not be displayed. The difference is that here, the browser will have recognised the tags as belonging to its area of knowledge.

Cancelling the instructions

In general, for every start tag there must be an end tag. However, some elements do not have any content, so an end tag does not exist. For example, the tag **
** will cause a line break: it is just an instruction, so there is no text formatting to cancel. Therefore, the end tag **</BR>** is prohibited.

In addition, some end tags can be omitted, and are said to be optional.

For example, the tag **<UL>** (Unordered List) starts a list that must be ended by **</UL>**. Within this element, every item of the list must start with the tag **<LI>**, and logic dictates that each item should end with **</LI>**.

A list of three lines could be coded as follows:

```
<UL><!—start list -->
<LI>Line 1</LI>
<LI>Line 2</LI>
```

```
<LI>Line 3</LI>
</UL><!--end list -->
```

However, the browser assumes that if it encounters the tag <LI>, then the preceding line must end with an implicit </LI>. Similarly, if it encounters the tag </UL> which closes the list, it will cancel the other tags included in it.

Therefore, the code

```
<UL>
<LI>Line 1
<LI>Line 2
<LI>Line 3
</UL>
```

will yield a perfectly functional list of three lines.

Furthermore, some end tags are not absolutely prohibited, and some elements can be used without the end tag or the start tag! As HTML, useful and efficient though it may be, is not completely standardised, it is impossible to guess which tags can or must be omitted.

Combining instructions on the same content

 Instructions can be combined to act on the same content.

For example, knowing that the tag <I> instructs the browser to start displaying text in italics, the text

The quick brown <B>fox</B> jumps over the lazy <B><I>dog</I></B>.

will be interpreted by the browser to display

The quick brown fox jumps over the lazy *dog*.

The word 'dog' will be displayed in both boldface and italics.

Note the order in which the instructions were closed according to the LIFO (last in, first out) principle: the last instruction given is the first to be closed. This is a rule to follow for 'clean' programming, even if the browser interpretation engine will tolerate variations. The rule is simple: when an element x contains an element y, the element y must be closed before the element x, or the contained element must be closed before the container element. This is usually referred to as 'nesting'.

2. Attributes: modifying elements

 An attribute can be considered to be a property of an element.

Some elements have a certain number of **attributes** which may be general or specific to that element.

For example, as the element **IMG** concerns images, we start an image field with the tag <IMG>. But this tag is not enough: you must tell the browser which image is involved.

The attribute **src** is used to specify the *SouRCe* of the image.

If the image to be displayed is contained in the file birmingham.gif, we will have to write the following code:

```
<IMG src="birmingham.gif">
```

The attribute is placed in the start tag of the element.

The attribute receives a **value** that follows the '=' sign.

The **value** must always be placed between quotation marks (single or double, it makes no difference). The quotation marks are optional if the value contains only characters (e.g. A–Z or a–z), numbers (0–9), the '–' sign or the full stop '.'; to make things easier, always enclose the attribute value within quotation marks.

The names of the attributes are not case-sensitive.

The existence of a space on either side of the '=' sign does not matter.

Attributes need not be 'closed': the end tag of the element cancels everything to do with that element.

The default border of an image may be enlarged.

<IMG SRC="REENTRY.jpg" BORDER=30>

(border=0: no border).

Combining attributes

The start tag of an element can be given as many attributes as necessary. If two or more attributes are contradictory, the last one prevails.

Example: for reasons impossible to understand, the author gave the tag two identical attributes, but with different values.

```
<IMG src="1.gif" src="2.gif">
```

The browser will not crash: the file "2.gif" will be displayed. The browser reads the code from left to right, so, of the two contradictory attributes, the rightmost one will prevail.

Another example of combining attributes, not contradictory but complementary this time:

```
<IMG src="1.gif" alt="This is an image
of a puma">
```

The attribute **alt** is an *alternative* to the image.

If you choose to use your browser without displaying images (so that pages are downloaded more quickly), if the browser is not capable of displaying images, or if it is unable to find the image, the alternative text (which is the value of the attribute) will be displayed in the space set aside for the image: the reader will at least receive this information.

Some browsers use the value of the attribute **alt** to display a ToolTip which appears when the mouse pointer passes over the image (or its location if the image is not displayed). This is an excellent way to document a link attached to a graphic button. For example, a button may indicate 'boats'. This example is probably a little unrealistic: if you click the button, you may find a catalogue or a 12,000-page thesis. The **alt** value can specify the nature of the contents linked to the button, for example:

'GoTo Bush, Vannevar. Article: 'As We May Think' – Atlantic Monthly 176, no 1' (1945).

GoTo Bush, Vannevar. Article : As We May Think.
Atlantic Monthly 176, no 1 (1945)

Order of attributes

 The order of attributes is important in certain cases.

The element **BODY** commences the body of the page; this element has two attributes:

>**bgcolor,** which is used to attribute a background colour generated by the system;

>**background,** which is used to display a background based on an image file.

The tag

<BODY bgcolor="#000000">

will paint the background of the page black (the value of **bgcolor** must be expressed in a hexadecimal number), while the tag

<BODY background="frame.gif">

will fill the background of the page with a mosaic of the image frame.gif.

The two attributes can be combined to give

```
<BODY bgcolor="#000000"
background="frame.gif">
```

or

```
<BODY background="frame.gif"
bgcolor="#000000">
```

With the first tag, the background will be painted black, then filled with the image; if the browser does not find the image, the background will still be painted black.

With the second tag, the background will be filled with the image then painted black. Whether the browser finds the image or not, the result in both these cases will be a black background.

Colours

The value of the attribute **color** can be expressed either as a hexadecimal number (prefixed by a hash symbol: #) or one of the names of the following 16 preset colours:

Names of colours and RGB values	
Black = "#000000"	**Maroon** = "#800000"
Green = "#008000"	**Navy** = "#000080"
Silver = "#C0C0C0"	**Red** = "#FF0000"
Lime = "#00FF00"	**Blue** = "#0000FF"
Gray = "#808080"	**Purple** = "#800080"
Olive = "#808000"	**Teal** = "#008080"
White = "#FFFFFF"	**Fuchsia** = "#FF00FF"
Yellow = "#FFFF00"	**Aqua** = "#00FFFF"

The value '#800080' and the value 'Purple' both refer to the same colour.

'Bgcolor=silver' is equivalent to 'Bgcolor=#C0C0C0'.

Event-driven attributes

To allow interactivity, most elements are sensitive to events generated by the user (e.g., a mouse click on the element). The event is detected by the browser, which hands the task over to a script. Not all elements support event-driven attributes.

Use the attribute	To produce the following effect
Onblur	The element has just been blurred.
Onchange	The element has undergone a change.
Onclick	A click was carried out on the element.
Ondblclick	A double click was carried out on the element.
Onfocus	The element has just been focused.

Onkeydown	A key is in down position.
Onkeypress	A key was pressed.
Onkeyup	A key was released.
Onload	The loading of the element is complete.
Onmousedown	The mouse button is pressed.
Onmousemove	The mouse pointer moves over the element.
Onmouseout	The mouse pointer has left the element.
Onmouseover	The mouse pointer is over the element.
Onmouseup	The mouse pointer has just been released.
Onreset	The element has just been reset.
Onselect	An item has just been selected in the element.

| Onsubmit | The form has just been sent to the server. |
| Onunload | The element was withdrawn from the browser interface. |

Blurred/focused

An element is focused [Focus] when it is designated to receive an action. For example, in a conventional dialogue box with two buttons (*OK* and *Cancel*), one of these buttons is focused by default: this is the button that will be pressed if you press Enter. If you use the tab key, the other button is enabled and is focused (highlighted) while the previous one is blurred [No Focus].

3. Conventions in this book

1

Elements are always noted in capitals: **TABLE**, TABLE and THEAD are elements. Boldface is irrelevant.

2

Even at the beginning of a line, **attributes** are noted in lowercase. Boldface is irrelevant: cols and **align** are both attributes.

3

The values that an attribute can assume are noted in lowercase and italics, even at the beginning of a line. These values may represent different types: *left* and *circle* are both values.

Values determined by the HTML standard

<ELEMENT align=*left|center|right*>

Meaning: the attribute **align** of the element ELEMENT can take one of the values *left*, *center* or *right* as in <TABLE align=*center*>.

Whole values

<ELEMENT width=*integer*>

Meaning: the attribute **width** of the element ELEMENT is an integer.

Figurative values

<TABLE width=*length*>

The *length* value can be expressed both as an integer representing a number of pixels and as a percentage of the space available on the output peripheral (screen, printer, etc.).

Thus, the value '60' means 60 pixels. The value '50%' means half the available horizontal space (between the margins, inside a table cell, etc.). For heights, the value '50%' means half the vertical space available (in the current window, in the current table cell, etc.).

Specialised values

Some attributes can assume a value only for a specific unit of measure. Thus:

border=pixels

means that the attribute **border** must receive a value expressed in pixels, and

<TABLE border=5>

starts the table with a border 5 pixels wide. In this case, the unit is understood by default, so it is not necessary to indicate it.

Color values

The value represented by *color* can be either a hexadecimal number like #000000, or a name, such as 'white'.

4. Writing HTML code

To write in HTML, you need a text editor capable of saving the document produced in 'text only' format, i.e. basic ASCII.

The file will be saved with the extension .HTM or .HTML, usable directly by a browser. The extension .HTM dates from the time when operating systems could not read more than three characters after the dot.

Most tags are not case-sensitive: <BODY>, <body>, <bODy> and all other variations are interpreted in the same way (but case does matter in complex characters: see Appendix 2). Nevertheless, it is a good idea to write tags in uppercase and attributes in lowercase.

The code can be entered by 'straight keying'; the browser will be able to interpret it, but you can create indents to make it easier for you to read.

For example, the code

```
<UL>
<LI>Line 1
<LI>Line 2
<LI>Line 3
</UL>
```

would be easier to read as:

```
<UL>
  <LI>Line 1
  <LI>Line 2
  <LI>Line 3
</UL>
```

but would function just as well as this:

```
<UL><LI>Line 1<LI>Line 2<LI>Line 3</UL>
```

5. Special characters

Because HTML reserves certain characters for use by the browser, it is necessary to express them as en **entity** (or escape sequence) if you want to use them in the content.

Example:

You want the following text to appear on a page:

The tag <TABLE> starts a table.

If you write the code like this

```
<HTML>
The tag <TABLE> starts a table.
</HTML>
```

the browser will display this:

The tag

starts a table.

The browser has interpreted the code to the letter:

- ❖ when it encountered <TABLE>, it started a table;
- ❖ it did not display the tag;
- ❖ in the absence of an end tag for the element TABLE, it included the rest of the content in the table.

 If you want to display reserved characters, you must express them as entities.

Thus:

- ❖ the character '<' will be represented by the entity **<**
- ❖ the character '>' will be represented by the entity **>**

So, to rewrite our code (ignore the boldface, it is used here to help you to distinguish the entities):

> <HTML>
> The tag **<**TABLE**>** starts a table.
> </HTML>

The browser will yield the desired text:

The tag <TABLE> starts a table.

⚠ An entity begins with '&' and ends with ';'.

Entities are also very useful for writing characters that are difficult to access from the keyboard; for example, the copyright symbol (©) matches the entity © and the entity & replaces the character '&'.

Any character can also be replaced by the entity which represents its position in the Unicode reference. This is very practical for including a character in a foreign alphabet. For example, the Unicode entity ا represents the Hebrew character aleph (א).

A wide range of characters is included in the Unicode, and all browsers are capable of interpreting them. The copyright symbol may be represented by © (HTML entity) or by © (Unicode entity). The coding can be written in decimal or in hexadecimal:

Character	HTML Entity	Decimal	Hexadecimal
Œ	&OElig;	&#338;	&#x152;

A list of entities for the most common complex characters is given in Appendix 2.

HTML documents: Web pages

STRUCTURE OF WEB PAGES

A document in HTML must comply with a very strict structure if it is to be truly universal, and capable of being used by any browser on any platform.

A Web page must have the following structure:

The **DOCTYPE** optional element, which is a declaration of the HTML version used for the document and its reference;

The **HTML** element, which contains the entire document;

the **HEAD** element, which contains information about the document (its title, information for search robots, etc.);

the **BODY** element, which is the content of the document (intended for the user).

```
<DOCTYPE>
<HTML>
<HEAD>...title and metadata ...</HEAD>
<BODY>...corpus...</BODY>
</HTML>
```

1. DOCTYPE
Declaration of the type of document

Ideally, the first line of the code of a document written in HTML should look like this:

```
<!DOCTYPE HTML PUBLIC "-//W3C//DTD
HTML 4.0//EN" "http://www.w3.org/-
TR/REC-html40/strict.dtd">
```

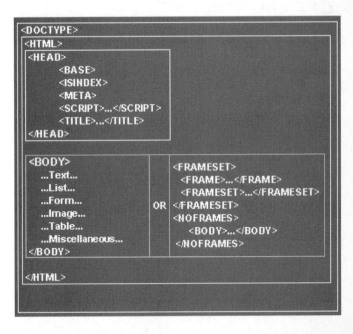

⚠ There is no end tag.

The declaration announces that this is an HTML **public** document, compliant with DTD HTML 4.0, and gives the URL where this standard can be found.

The page will still be usable if this element is missing.

2. HTML and /HTML
Declaration of the nature of the document

This element does not have attributes. It is used to inform browsers about the nature of the document. These tags are now obsolete and optional: browsers recognise a Web page from the extension of the file that contains it (.HTM or .HTML).

3. HEAD and /HEAD
Document head

This element can contain various optional elements which, if used, must appear in the following order:

**\<BASE>\<ISINDEX>\<LINK>\<META>\<SCRIPT>
\<TITLE>**

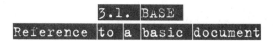

3.1. BASE
Reference to a basic document

\<base href="http://jump.altavista.com/">

This element is used to indicate the basic document (name and location) for resolving links that refer to locations within the current document. In practice, this element will be used only if the same document has different URLs (which is the case, for example, with the homepages of search engines like AltaVista and Yahoo!) or if the document does not have an URL (e.g., an

HTML document sent by e-mail). The document could even be used offline.

The BASE element has two attributes:

✔ **href** — which gives the URL of the basic document concerned;

✔ **target** — which indicates the default destination framework of documents invoked by lines (this attribute is used only if the document has frames).

3.2. ISINDEX
Access to an index

This element is now obsolete and has been replaced by the simple element **INPUT**, to mark the existence of an index and display a text box to introduce a keyword.

3.3. LINK
Definition of relationships between documents

The attribute **REL** of this element defines the relationship between the document which contains the element and the document to which it links. The attribute **REV** defines the reverse relationship.

Examples:

<LINK REL=Glossary HREF="glos.html">
means that the document glos.html is a satellite of the current document, whereas

<LINK REV=Chapter HREF="work.html">
means that the current document is a chapter within the document work.html.

This element is used to include the document that precedes the current document in a sequence, the next document, the starting page, a copyright page, a page about the author, etc.

Example:

```
<LINK REL=Start HREF="../" TITLE="Quick
HTML">

<LINK REL=Prev HREF="bas06.html"
TITLE="IsIndex">

<LINK REL=Next HREF="bas08.html"
TITLE="Metadata">

<LINK REL=Copyright HREF=
"/copyright.html" TITLE="Copyright">

<LINK REV=Made HREF=
"boss@argwal.com" TITLE="Feedback">
```

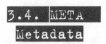

3.4. META
Metadata

The META element stores metadata (keywords about
the document, author, etc.) that can be used by search
robots. As these robots use an open-ended and non-

standard list of attributes, the Web page designer may draw inspiration from the examples below. Here, the title of the attribute is NAME, while the value of the attribute is CONTENT:

> **<META NAME="author" CONTENT="Aya Redone">**
>
> **<META NAME="description" CONTENT= "One of the best presentations of HTML 4.0">**
>
> **<META NAME="keywords" CONTENT=" HyperText, HyperText Markup Language, HTML, HTML4, HTML 4.0">**

 Search engines tend to cut the 'description' to about 200 characters.

Search engines take account of case in the keywords, they do not index the document if the same keyword is found too often (regardless of case), and they process only the first 1,000 characters.

Some search engines also take into account the attribute **robots**.

<META NAME="robots" CONTENT="">

CONTENT could take the following values:

index
> the page should be indexed;

noindex
> the page should not be indexed;

follow
> the robot should follow the links on the page that point to other pages, which should also be indexed;

nofollow
> the opposite of follow;

all
> means index, follow (default value);

none
>   means noindex, nofollow.

All combinations are possible, but you must separate the values with a comma:

> **<META NAME=robots CONTENT="noindex, follow">**

This means: no index, but follow the links.

The attribute **http-equiv** presents other facilities offered by certain servers:

➥ notify the browser that it must use its interpretation module for JavaScript:

> **<META HTTP-EQUIV="Content-Script-Type" CONTENT="text/javascript">;**

➥ fix an expiry date for the document:

> **<META HTTP-EQUIV="Expires" CONTENT= "Sun, 22 Mar 2000 14:16:00 GMT">;**

- notify the browser that style sheets are used:

  <META HTTP-EQUIV="Content-Style-Type"
  CONTENT="text/css">

- force the browser to load another Web page after
  a certain period (here, 20 seconds):

  <META HTTP-EQUIV="Refresh" CONTENT=
  "20; URL=http://www.argwal.com/">.

Note

Some search engines do not index pages that use too short
a REFRESH function, and some browsers do not recognise this
command, despite the fact it is part of the official HTML
reference.

3.5 SCRIPT and /SCRIPT
Integrated mini-programs

This element specifies a mini-program integrated into the document. Scripts in JavaScript or VBScript are used to make the document more interactive, so that it can include features such as a multiple-choice form which will continue to function even if the user saves the page and uses it offline.

The script language must be declared:

<SCRIPT LANGUAGE="JavaScript">.

⚠ This declaration is obsolete and should be replaced by:

<SCRIPT TYPE="text/javascript">.

If a module outside the page is needed, it must be indicated as follows:

<SCRIPT TYPE="text/javascript" SRC="aya.js">.

If the browser does not succeed in loading the source, it will ignore the script. It is best to provide an alternative script, included in the page, and instruct the browser accordingly:

```
<SCRIPT TYPE="text/javascript"
SRC="aya.js" CHARSET="ISO-8859-1">    1

<!--// alternative script to use if the module
aya.js cannot be found // -->

</SCRIPT>.    2
```

The attribute **charset** indicates the standard used to write the module "aya.js". If the browser does not find this standard (1), it will switch to the alternative script (2), also included in the page, and thus available: the user will not receive an error message.

Another way to avoid the problems caused if a script fails to function is to provide an alternative by means of the **NOSCRIPT** element:

> **<NOSCRIPT>...</NOSCRIPT> Alternative to a script.**

If the browser proves incapable of running a script, the **NOSCRIPT** element specifies the alternative content to present to the user. This element must follow directly after the script it concerns.

Usually, the **SCRIPT** element is placed in the HEAD element, but it can also appear in the BODY element.

Don't be afraid of JavaScript: use it to open your documents in a sized window! Just save this code in a text only file.

```
<HTML><HEAD>
<script language="JavaScript">
<!--
```

```
function openWindow(url) {
popupWin = window.open(url, "remote",
"width=300,height=200")
}
// -->
</script>
</HEAD>
<BODY LINK="#FFFF00">
<FONT FACE="ARIAL" SIZE=6>
Open a sized window.

<BR>

<a href=
"javascript:openWindow("DocumentToDisplay.
html");">Open a sized Window.</a>

</BODY>

</HTML>
```

A click on the link will open a window sized in 300 by 200 pixels.

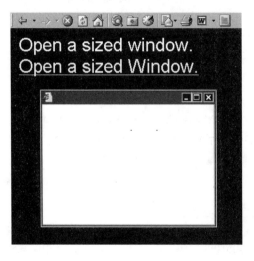

3.6. TITLE and /TITLE
Document title

`<title>Greenwich - Search</title>`

This element defines the title of the document, i.e. the text that will appear:

- in the browser title bar;
- in the Windows taskbar if the document is minimised or masked;
- in the browser's History;
- in the list yielded by search engines (e.g., AltaVista, Yahoo!, etc.).

As space is limited in the first three objects capable of displaying them (the browser title bar, Windows taskbar and browser's history), titles must be short and explicit.

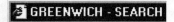

> **HERE COMES THE CONTENTS OF THE TITLE ELEMENT**

The title of the document appears in the browser title bar and History, and in the Windows taskbar.

```
<HTML>
<HEAD>
<TITLE>HERE COMES THE CONTENTS OF
THE TITLE ELEMENT</TITLE>
</HEAD>
<BODY></BODY></HTML>
```

4. BODY and /BODY
Document body

The BODY element contains the content of the document (the part intended to be shown or used): the text, lists, images, sounds, links and other objects.

Some objects may constitute an integral part of the document, in two forms:

- the object may have a *real* presence in the document; for example, the text to display, which can be read by consulting the code of the document;

- the object may have a *virtual* presence: the document comprises only the code needed for the object to be created by the browser, (e.g. the tag <INPUT> obliges the browser to display a text field).

Other objects are simply attached to the document by **links**; the code contains a description of these links (URLs), but not the objects themselves. This is the case with images, for example.

The background is filled with a uniform colour:

```
<BODY BGCOLOR=silver>
```

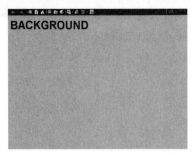

In the next example, the background of the browser's window is filled by a mosaic (a small image automatically repeated).

```
<BODY BACKGROUND="misc026.gif">
```

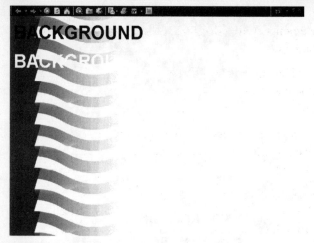

Take care with the contrast between background and font colors.

The BODY element contains *inline* elements and *block* elements. They are usually displayed at the beginning of a new line.

The inline elements contain text and other inline elements. When displayed, these elements do not start a new line.

This information can give an idea of the structure of a document in HTML (see page 68 and Appendix 1, page 197).

Some elements can be considered to be blocks, while others can be used either as blocks or as inline elements.

This is very important in style sheets, and we follow the rule that an element used inline cannot contain block-level elements. Appendix 1 shows which elements belong to which level.

In a document containing frames, the BODY element is replaced by the **FRAMESET** element.

Block				
	inline			
		text		
	Block			
		inline		
			text	
			inline	
				text
		inline		
			text	

3

Links
and anchors

Links and anchors

An **HTML link** is a connection between one Web resource and another.

Logically, a link must have two ends:

- The **source document:** this is the **anchor**, which contains the type, name and location of the linked resource;

- The **resource** to be invoked, which is defined in the anchor: this is the **target** of the link (e.g., an image, a video clip, another HTML document, an anchor in another document, a bookmark in the source document, a file, etc.).

An anchor is the content of a particular **element**, an area inside the HTML document. This area can include text or another object, and it is therefore possible to put a link on text, on an image, and by means of a script, on any other element.

Elements which define links

Two HTML elements define links: **LINK** and **A**.

A **LINK** element can appear only in the **HEAD** element; it defines the relationships between the current document and other resources (see *rel* and *rev*).

The **A** element is placed in the **BODY** of a document.

The links are usually identified by colour (for text) or by a border (for an image). A link can be activated by clicking with the mouse or by a voice command.

`<P><IMG SRC="acamain.gif">`

`<P><A HREF="nextpage.html"><IMG SRC="acamain.gif"></A>`

The browser interprets this activation as an order to go and find the target resource of this link, and if it finds it, it will use it according to the nature of the target: a document in HTML will be displayed, or the resource will be handled by a program outside the browser or by a plug-in integrated into the browser.

The attribute **title** of the **A** element could be used to add information about the nature of the link. This information may be represented by a help bubble, or it may change the appearance of the cursor, etc.

A and /A

The **A** element defines an **anchor,** an anchoring of a resource in the current document. This is where the links begin to step in.

 An A element cannot contain another A element.

The attribute **href** defines the **URL** of the resource:

```
<A HREF="photos.html">My private photo
album</A>

<A HREF="../images/woody.jpg">Picture of
my dog</A>
```

```
<A HREF="http://www.argwal.com/sounds
/music.mid" TYPE="audio/midi" ACCESS-
KEY=A>Piece of music in MIDI format (10
KB)</A>
```

The attribute **type** specifies the link medium, which saves the browser having to download a resource it would be incapable of using.

The attribute **title** is used to give a brief description of the content of the link; its value is displayed as a ToolTip by certain browsers.

Some browsers automatically use the TITLE as the subject of the message if the link relates to e-mail:

```
<A HREF="mailto:ayaredone@argwal.com"
TITLE="Feedback on HTML overview">
FEEDBACK</A>
```

The value of the attribute **title** could be read out by a voice user agent, or represented by a ToolTip.

The attribute **target** is used with framed documents to specify the name (i.e., the value of the attribute **name**) of the destination frame of the link:

```
<A HREF="chapter2.html" target="main"
title="II. Common Objects">Chapter 2</A>
```

Some values of the attribute target have a particular meaning:	
_blank	displays the resource invoked in a new unnamed window;
_self	displays the resource invoked in the frame of the invoking link;
_parent	displays the resource in the parent FRAMESET;
_top	displays the resource invoked in the container window.

The attribute **lang** specifies the language to use for the encoding: *en* (English), *fr* (French), *en-US* (American English), *ja* (Japanese), etc. The attribute **charset** specifies the type of character set: *ISO-8859-1*, *SHIFT_JIS* or *UTF-8*.

The attribute **accesskey** specifies a single character which will be used as a keyboard shortcut to activate the link.

The attribute **tabindex** gives the rank of the element in the tabulation order (0–32767).

The attributes **rel** and **rev** define the relations between the anchor and the linked source.

The attributes **shape** and **coords** are for use with an image on which clickable areas have been specified.

The different shape values	
rect	Default value. Determines a rectangular area defined with COORDS="left / top / right / bottom".
default	The entire image forms a single clickable area.
circle	Determines a circular area defined with COORDS= "center-x / center-y / radius".
poly	Determines a polygonal area defined with COORDS="x1 / y1 / x2 / y2 /xN / yN".

The values of the attribute **coords** can be expressed in pixels or in percentages of dimension of the image considered. The origin of the measurements is the upper left-hand corner of the image (x=0, y=0).

The **A** element supports the event-driven attributes.

A link makes text underlined

Normal link : the text is underlined.

You may opt for an embedded style sheet, so that there will be no underlined links.

Incorporate these lines into your documents:
```
<HTML>
<HEAD>
<style>
```

```
<!--
a{text-decoration:none}
//-->
</style>
</HEAD>
<BODY>
<A HREF="doc1.html">Normal link: the text
is underlined.
</BODY>
</HTML>
```

4

Document objects

DOCUMENT OBJECTS

The document may contain different types of objects, such as text, images, lists, files, forms, scripts, etc. Despite the predominance of images on the Web, text remains the most common object in documents.

1. Text

Text is the main object of Web pages: indeed, HTML was initially designed for text. Text can be formatted by means of elements to present a page layout on screen.

Text variations

`<B>Bold text</B>`

`<BR><U>Underlined text</U>`

`<BR><I>Italic</I>`

`<BR>Normal and <sup>Superscript</sup> text`

`<BR>Normal and <sub>Subscript</sub> text`

`<BR><S>Strikethrough text</S>`

`<FONT FACE ="ARIAL" SIZE=7>`

`<BR><TT>Monospaced text</TT>`

Bold text

<u>Underlined text</u>

Italic

Normal and ^{Superscript} text

Normal and $_{Subscript}$ text

~~Strike through text~~

`Monospaced text`

Elements dedicated to fonts

···

<BASEFONT>
Changes the font

This element is used to change the typeface, size and colour of fonts. It affects all the text that follows its start tag, except for the heads (H1, H2, etc.). Some browsers do not interpret this element correctly for tables.

> ARIAL
>
> GARAMOND
>
> VERDANA
>
> TIMES

✔ The attribute **size** changes the size of characters on a scale of 1–7.

✔ The attribute **color** changes the colour of the text.

✔ The attribute **face** changes the typeface (Arial, Times, etc.).

ARIAL Size=1

GARAMOND Size=3

VERDANA Size=5

TIMES Size=7

....
<FONT>...</FONT>
Specifies the font

This element is used to set the typeface, size and colour of the font. It should be abandoned in favour of style sheets.

✔ The attribute **face** gives a list of fonts to be used by the browser in order of preference:

<FONT face= "Arial, Verdana, Times" size="4" color="#000000">

 If the browser does not find the first font on the user's system, it will search for the second, and so on.

✔ The attribute **color** determines the colour of the text. Some browsers do not interpret this attribute correctly.

✔ The attribute **size** fixes the size of the font on a scale from *1* to 7.

<FONT FACE="ARIAL" SIZE=7>
<P>Size 7
<FONT FACE="ARIAL" SIZE=6>
<P>Size 6
<FONT FACE="ARIAL" SIZE=5>

```
<P>Size 5
<FONT FACE="ARIAL" SIZE=4>
<P>Size 4
<FONT FACE="ARIAL" SIZE=3>
<P>Size 3
<FONT FACE="ARIAL" SIZE=2>
<P>Size 2
<FONT FACE="ARIAL" SIZE=1>
<P>Size 1
```

A size relative to that specified in the BASEFONT element can be specified (e.g. "size=+3" or "size=-1"), but this method invariably leads to problems.

Size 7

Size 6

Size 5

Size 4

Size 3

Size 2

Size 1

The seven sizes of text
(attribute Size for the element FONT).

Other tags dedicated to characters		
Keyword	**Effect**	**Tag**
B	Boldface	`<B></B>`
BIG	Large text	`<BIG></BIG>`
I	Italics	`<I></I>`
S	Strikethrough text	`<S></S>`
SMALL	Small text	`<SMALL></SMALL>`
STRIKE	Same as S	`<STRIKE></STRIKE>`
SUB	Subscript	`<SUB></SUB>`
SUP	Superscript	`<SUP></SUP>`
TT	Typewriter (fixed-width)	`<TT></TT>`
U	Underline	`<U></U>`

Elements applied to sentences

....

<ABBR>...</ABBR>

Abbreviation.

This element identifies abbreviations.

✔ The attribute **title** contains the non-abbreviated text and the book title as a ToolTip.

✔ If the abbreviated form is a pronounceable word, the **ACRONYM** element is used instead.

Examples:

<ABBR TITLE="United States of America">U.S.A.</ABBR>

<ACRONYM TITLE="North Atlantic Treaty Organization">NATO</ACRONYM>

`<ACRONYM>...</ACRONYM>`
Abbreviation pronounced as a word

This element functions like the element ABBR, but is dedicated to acronyms (pronounceable abbreviations).

> `<ACRONYM TITLE="Radio detecting and ranging">radar</ACRONYM>`

The abbreviation 'radar' can be pronounced as a word, whereas the abbreviation FBI must be pronounced letter by letter, and therefore must be identified by the ABBR element.

`<ADDRESS>...</ADDRESS>`
Contact address

> `<ADDRESS>Maintained by <A HREF="Webmaster.HTML"> NAME</A><A HREF="mailto:xxx"</A></ADDRESS>`

....
<BDO>...</BDO>
Text direction reversal

✔ The attribute **dir** specifies the direction to set for the text contained in that element:

<BDO dir=ltr>text</BDO> or <BDO dir=rtl>text</BDO>

text left to right

tfel ot thgir txet

The start tag can be replaced by the character ‭ (="rtl") or ‮ (="ltr"); the character ‬ can replace the end tag. These Unicode characters can be used with the attribute **dir**.

....

Forces a line break in the current text

✔ The attribute **clear** (values: *left* or *right*) is used to clear the rest of the text beyond 'floating objects' (tables, images, etc.):

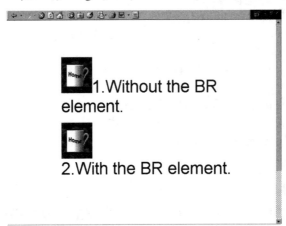

'BR' means 'break + carriage return'

1. <IMG SRC="home.jpg">1.Without the BR element.

2. <IMG SRC="home.jpg">
2.With the BR element.

....

<CITE>...</CITE>
Title reference

In a text, excerpts borrowed from other texts are usually written in italics: they are included in an **<I>** element. The **CITE** element will cause text to be displayed in italics, but it must be used only for the names of authors, magazines, newspapers, boats, etc., i.e. everything that one day could be referenced by a good search engine.

Example:

<CITE>Aya Redone</CITE> gave a brilliant review of the movie <CITE>The Last

Dance</CITE> yesterday in <CITE> The
Wezembeek Clarion</CITE>

If page designers use the CITE element judiciously and
systematically, this could serve to emphasise the authors,
for example.

....
<CODE>...</CODE>
Computer code

The browser displays the content of the **CODE**
element in *typewriter (fixed-width)* text, as the **TT**
element would do. As the spacing is very important
in computer code, it is best to surround the element
code with a **PRE** element, so as not form a chain of
multiple spaces.

Example with a PRE container element:

```
<PRE><CODE>

class HelloWorlds {public static void
main(String args) {System.out.println("Hello
Worlds!");}}

</CODE></PRE>
```

....

<DEL>...</DEL>
Deleted text

This element contains text that was deleted. It is used to memorise changes made from one version of the document to another. With a style sheet, the author can get the browser to display deletions as strikethrough text, or in another colour, or with a different intonation if the browser is capable of voice synthesis.

✔ The attribute **cite** is used to link to a document explaining the change.

✔ The attribute **title** could specify a shortcut to the explanation, which the browser will display in a ToolTip.

✔ The attribute **datetime** specifies the date and time of the deletion:

```
<DEL CITE="http://www.argwal.com/
changes.html" DATETIME="2000-12-19T03::
00-05:00" TITLE="MONEY is obsolete">
<P>The MONEY instruction changes to
RESOURCES.</P></DEL>
```

....
<EM>...</EM>
Emphasis

This element places emphasis on its content, which the browser translates into italics.

....

<H1>...</H1> --> <H6>...</H6>

Heading levels

The H1 element defines the main heading in a text. The elements H2 to H6 define levels of hierarchy.

Browsers usually interpret these elements by displaying the text they contain in boldface. Style sheets offer other possibilities.

Example:

```
h1 {
   color: #c33;
   background: transparent;
   font-weight: bold;
   text-align: center
}
h2 {
   color: #00008b;
```

```
background: transparent;
font-weight: bold;
margin-left: 2%;
margin-right: 2%
}
```

HEADING H1

HEADING H2

HEADING H3

HEADING H4

HEADING H5

HEADING H6

The six sizes for headings (elements H1 to H6)

....
<HR>
Horizontal line

Attributes	
align=[*left*|*center*|*right*]	horizontal alignment
noshade	full line
size=Pixels	thickness
width=Length	length

<CENTER>
<P>HR: horizontal rule.
<P>1. Default.
<HR>
<P>2. Fixed size (in percentage of the browser's window).

```
<HR WIDTH=70%>
<P>3. Left-aligned <I>in a Center
Element</I>.
<HR WIDTH=70% ALIGN="left">
</CENTER>
```

First, design a 1 by 1 pixel GIF or JPG image in the color you want. Then use the HTML codes below:

```
<img src="GreyDot.gif" width="300"
height="10">
```

This produces a horizontal line 300 pixels wide by 10 pixels high.

....

\<INS>...\</INS>

Inserted text

This element contains an addition to the original text. It is therefore used like the DEL element, whose attributes it shares, to keep track of the different changes made to a document.

....

\<KBD>...\</KBD>

Text entered by the user

This element specifies the text that was entered by the user, which the browser translates by displaying typewriter (fixed-width) text (as if this text were contained in the TT element):

```
<P>If the material does not exist,
enter <KBD>Not Available</KBD>.
```

....

<P>...</P>
Paragraph

The browser usually displays the content of this element without an indented first line, after inserting a blank line. However, some browsers allow the user to define the layout of paragraphs.

In a style sheet, the layout can be set by applying the following rule:

```
P { margin-top: 0; text-indent: 5% }
```

....

<PRE>...</PRE>
Preformatted text

This element is used to display correctly text whose formatting is important (software code, a poem, etc.). The browser usually treats different characteristics of the text in certain ways (it closes up multiple spaces, cuts lines according to the horizontal space available, etc.), which this element prohibits.

<SAMP>...</SAMP>
Sample text

This element contains a sample text, which the browser displays in typewriter (fixed-width) font.

<P>Courtesy: when you are asked how you are, answer: </P>

<P><SAMP>How are you?</SAMP></P>

<STRONG>...</STRONG>
Strong emphasis

The browser translates this element by displaying the text concerned in boldface.

<VAR>...</VAR>
Variables or arguments

This element contains the variables and arguments of the software. The browser displays them in italics.

<P>Software versions are usually numbered using the following format: <VAR>x</VAR>.<VAR>x</VAR></P>

2. Lists

<DIR>...</DIR>
  List

This element creates a simple list. Each line of this list is contained in an **LI** element.

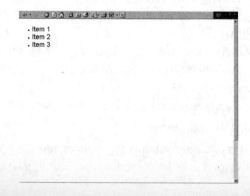

The attribute **compact** forces the browser to display the list in the most compact form possible.

To create a list, it is better to use **UL** or **OL**.

....

<DL>...</DL>
List of definitions

This element creates a list of terms and their definitions. The **DT** element contains the element to define, the **DD** element contains the definition. The same term can have

- Item 1
- Item 2
- Item 3

several definitions, or no definition at all. Several terms may have the same definition. It is even possible to code a definition in anticipation of a term.

```
<DL>
<DT>ELEMENT TO DEFINE 1 (D1)</DT>
<DD>
```

```
    <P>DEFINITION 1 for D1
    <P>DEFINITION 2 for D1</P>
    </DD>
    <DT>ELEMENT TO DEFINE 2 (D2)</DT>
    <DT>ELEMENT TO DEFINE 3 (D3)</DT>
    <DD>
     <P>DEFINITION for D3</P>
     </DD>
     </DL>
```

....

<DT>...</DT>

Term to define in a DL list

This element contains a term to define in a list of definitions.

 The end tag is optional, but it is best to include it to avoid confusing certain browsers.

`<DD>...</DD>`
Definition of a term in a DL list

This element gives the definition of a term contained in a DT element of a list of definitions.

 The end tag is optional, but it is best to include it to avoid confusing certain browsers.

`<LI>...</LI>`
List item

This element defines an item in the **DIR, MENU, OL** and **UL** elements. For instance, this is a list with 3 items:

`<UL><LI>Item 1<LI>Item 2<LI>Item 3<UL>`.

An **LI** element can contain a UL or OL element:

`<UL><LI>Item 1<LI>Item 2<UL><LI>Item 2.1<LI>Item 2.2</UL><LI>Item 3</UL>`.

It is thus possible to create multi-level trees marked by an indent.

By default, the browser attributes a different type of bullet to each level.

The bullets can be set by the attribute **type**, which may take the following values.

Value	Effect on bullet
In a UL, DIR or MENU list:	
Type="disc"	Disk full
Type="square"	Hollow square
Type="circle"	Circle
In an OL list:	
Type="1"	Decimal number
Type="a"	Lowercase character
Type="A"	Uppercase alphabetic character
Type="I"	Lowercase Roman numeral
Type="I"	Uppercase Roman numeral

Note

Style sheets provide greater flexibility, including the ability to use images as bullets in lists, and to delete bullets.

\<MENU>...\</MENU>
List

This element defines a list of the items which are **LI** elements.

• Item 1
• Item 2
• Item 3

The MENU list = the DIR list.

The attribute **compact** forces the browser to display the list in the most compact form possible.

To create a list, it is better to use **UL** or **OL**.

••••••••••••••••••••••••••••••

`<OL>...</OL>`
Ordered list

1. **Item 1**
2. **Item 2**
3. **Item 3**

This element defines a list, each item of which is contained in an **LI** element.

Unlike the 'unordered' **UL** list, the items of the **OL** list are in a defined sequence, so each item is numbered. The number bullet can be determined by the attribute type (see the **LI** element).

✔ The value of the attribute **start** forces the browser to start the sequence at a given number.

✔ The attribute **compact** forces the browser to display the list in the most compact form possible.

....
\<UL>...\</UL>
Unordered list

This element creates a list where each of the items is contained in an **LI** element. The items are not part of a sequence. By default, the browser puts a bullet in front of each item. The type of bullet (disk, square or circle) can be determined by the attribute type (see the **LI** element).

- **Item 1**
- **Item 2**
- **Item 3**

- **Item 1**
- **Item 2**
- **Item 3**

○ **Item 1**
○ **Item 2**
○ **Item 3**

Type ="disk"   Type="square"   Type="circle"

✔ The attribute **compact** forces the browser to display the list in the most compact form possible.

3. Forms

\<FORM\>...\</FORM\>
Interactive form

This element defines a form, whose different elements (also known as *controls* in this case) ensure interactivity between the user of the page and the server.

Before the form is submitted, the data entered in the form can be verified automatically by means of a local script (included in the page), and certain constraints may be imposed on the user (e.g., not to enter text longer than n characters). To submit (send) the form to the server, you must use either a **BUTTON** element or an **INPUT** element. The nature of this action is specified by the value of the attribute **ACTION**.

When the form arrives at the server, it is processed by a script written in CGI or Java (such a program is known as a servlet or 'mini-application for the server', but this is beyond the scope of this book).

There are very many scripts available for processing forms at the server end.

....
<BUTTON>...</BUTTON>
Button

The BUTTON element is created by the start tag <BUTTON>.

✔ The value of the attribute **type** specifies whether it is a *submit* button (to send the form to the server), *reset* (to reset the form by clearing all the information entered in it) or *button* (to use this button in a script).

✔ The attribute **accesskey** specifies a single character that can serve as a shortcut key for the button.

✔ The attribute **disabled** disables the button and withdraws it from the field of action (it can no longer be focused, and tabulation ignores it as if it no longer existed).

✔ The attribute **tabindex** specifies the rank of the button (between 0 and 32767) in the tabulation order.

The BUTTON element can also be used by local scripts. To this end, it responds to **standard events** and two other events: ONFOCUS (the button has just been focused) and ONBLUR (the button has just been blurred).

✔ The attribute **value** will be used to label the button.

✔ The attribute **alt** specifies the text that will be displayed if the browser cannot load the image.

```
<INPUT type="image" SRC="but.gif"
ALT="Send">.
```

✔ The value *image* of the attribute **type** is used to introduce an image in the button.

✔ The value *button* of the attribute **type** defines a standard pushbutton that can be used for local scripts. The attribute value fixes the label of the button. Event-driven attributes (**onclick, onmouseon**, etc.) will be used to manage the interactivity.

1.
2.
3.
4.
5.

Simple buttons for the script

....

<INPUT>
Text input field

This element creates a field in which you can input text.

The HTML standard lets you place an INPUT element anywhere on the page, but some browsers do not recognise this element outside a form.

Input box : [Enter your text here]

✔ The attribute **name** is used to identify the element at the server, when it receives the form.

✔ The attribute **value** specifies the initial content of the element, which, by analogy, can suggest content to the user.

✔ The attribute **size** specifies the number of characters for the entry.

✔ The attribute **maxlength** specifies the maximum number of characters to be accepted during the input. This attribute does not constitute a foolproof way to discourage verbose users: as this limit is imposed at the client end, a user can edit the document, increase the value of maxlength and send twelve million characters to the server! It is therefore necessary to double this attribute by its counterpart on the server end.

✔ The attribute **readonly** prevents the user from editing the content of the element.

✔ The attribute **disabled** disables the element. If the attribute **readonly** is present, the content of the element will not be transmitted when the form is submitted to the server.

✔ The attribute **type** can be *text* or *password*. The default value of the attribute is *text*. It can be given the value *password*: the characters entered are then masked and replaced by asterisks. Note that such a password is transmitted in plain text, and is therefore not secure for financial transactions, etc.

Input box with Type="password":

```
**********************
```

✔ The attribute **type** can also take the values *radio* and *checkbox*, which are on/off switches.

```
<P>Please indicate your preference for
payment:</P>

<P><LABEL ACCESSKEY=C><INPUT
TYPE=radio NAME="payment" VALUE=
"credit card" CHECKED> Credit
card</LABEL><BR>

<LABEL ACCESSKEY=M><INPUT
TYPE=radio NAME="payment"
VALUE="nature"> Nature</LABEL></P>
<P><LABEL ACCESSKEY=S><INPUT
TYPE=checkbox NAME="send" VALUE=
"yes" CHECKED> Send receipt by e-mail?
</LABEL></P>
```

Please indicate your preference for payment:

⊙ Credit card
○ cash

☑ Send receipt by e-mail ?

⚠ As the three radio button **INPUT** elements were given the same **NAME**, it will be impossible to tick more than one at a time.

Resetting the form

✔ The value *reset* of the attribute **type** obliges the **INPUT** element to create a button that will be used only to reset the initial values of the form.

Submitting the form to the server

✔ The attribute **type** can also take the value *submit*. The button is then used to submit (send) the form to the server.

Note

In addition to the standard event-driven attributes, the **INPUT** element accepts the following event-driven attributes:

onfocus	the element has just been focused;
onblur	the element has just been blurred;
onselect	the text of the element (text or password) has just been selected;
onchange	the content of the element has changed, and it has just been blurred.

...

<SELECT>...</SELECT>
List of options

This element creates a list of options that can be selected separately or by multiple selection. It can be placed anywhere on the page, but some browsers do not recognise it outside a form.

The **SELECT** element contains one or more **OPTGROUP** or **OPTION** elements to organise a list of options. The **OPTION** element contains one option. The **OPTGROUP** element contains one or more **OPTION** elements.

✔ The attribute **name** specifies the key that will be sent to the server with the value of the selected option.

✔ The Boolean attribute **multiple** is used for multi-selection:

```
<FONT FACE="ARIAL" SIZE="3">
<P>Select one or more sections to search:
<P><SELECT NAME=MULTIPLE>
<OPTION>Official Reference</OPTION>
<OPTION>FAQ</OPTION>
<OPTION>Good old Y2K</OPTION>
<OPTION>Tools</OPTION>
<OPTION>Press</OPTION>
</SELECT>
</P>
```

Select one or more sections to search :

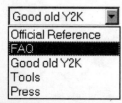

✔ The attribute **disabled** disables the element.

✔ The value of the attribute **tabindex** ranks the element in the tabulation order (between *0* and *32767*).

The element **SELECT** reacts to events; in addition to the standard event-driven attributes, it has the attributes **onfocus**, **onblur** and **onchange**.

....
<OPTGROUP>...</OPTGROUP>
Option group

This element contains one or more **OPTION** elements in a **SELECT** menu element.

The attribute **label** describes the group to the user. Cascading menus are then provided. Some browsers cannot interpret this element: they will display only the OPTION element.

```html
<P>Which browser do you want to use?
<SELECT NAME=browser>
<OPTGROUP LABEL="Netscape
Navigator">
<OPTION LABEL="4.x or higher">
Netscape Navigator 4.x or higher
</OPTION>
<OPTION LABEL="3.x">Netscape
Navigator 3.x</OPTION>
<OPTION LABEL="2.x">Netscape
Navigator 2.x</OPTION>
<OPTION LABEL="1.x">Netscape
Navigator 1.x</OPTION>
</OPTGROUP>
<OPTGROUP LABEL="Microsoft Internet
Explorer">
<OPTION LABEL="4.x or higher">
Microsoft Internet Explorer 4.x or higher
```

```
  </OPTION>
  <OPTION LABEL="3.x">Microsoft
Internet Explorer 3.x</OPTION>
  <OPTION LABEL="2.x">Microsoft
Internet Explorer 2.x</OPTION>
  <OPTION LABEL="1.x">Microsoft
Internet Explorer 1.x</OPTION>
  </OPTGROUP>
  <OPTGROUP LABEL="Opera">
  <OPTION LABEL="3.x or higher">Opera
3.x or higher</OPTION>
  <OPTION LABEL="2.x">Opera
2.x</OPTION>
  </OPTGROUP>
  <OPTION>Other</OPTION>
  </SELECT>
 </P>
```

Which Web browser do you use most often?

Netscape Navigator 4.x or higher ▼
Netscape Navigator 4.x or higher
Netscape Navigator 3.x
Netscape Navigator 2.x
Netscape Navigator 1.x
Microsoft Internet Explorer 4.x or higher
Microsoft Internet Explorer 3.x
Microsoft Internet Explorer 2.x
Microsoft Internet Explorer 1.x
Opera 3.x or higher
Opera 2.x
Other

The Boolean attribute **disabled** disables the element.

<OPTION>...</OPTION>
Option in a SELECT menu

This element specifies a choice in the **SELECT** element menu.

✔ The attribute **value** determines the value of the element (which will be sent to the server).

✔ The attribute **label** defines a label for the user.

✔ The attribute **selected** determines that the option will be selected when the menu is opened. Even when multiple selection is possible, only one option can be selected when the menu is opened.

✔ The Boolean attribute **disabled** disables the element.

....
<TEXTAREA>...</TEXTAREA>
Text area

Enter your name

in this Text area

| Enter your name here |

This element creates an area in which you can enter several lines of text. According to HTML specifications, it can be anywhere on the Web page, but some browsers do not recognise it outside a form.

✔ The initial value of the element (attribute **value**) cannot contain tags.

✔ The attribute **name** determines the identifier of the element.

✔ The attributes **rows** and **cols** determine the number of visible rows and columns.

✔ The attribute **accesskey** determines a simple character that will serve as a shortcut key to focus the element.

✔ The attribute **tabindex** determines the order of the element in the tabulation.

The **TEXTAREA** element reacts to the events; in addition to the standard event-driven attributes, it has the attributes **onblur**, **onchange** and **onselect**.

<FIELDSET>...</FIELDSET>
Groups certain controls of a form

This element is used to constitute groups of controls in a form.

A **FIELDSET** element must start with the identifier of the group of controls it is going to include: this is the **LEGEND** element. After this element, the FIELDSET element can contain any element, including another FIELDSET.

....
<LEGEND>...</LEGEND>
Name of a group of fields

This element defines a legend for the group formed by the controls of a **FIELDSET** element.

✔ The attribute **accesskey** specifies a single character that can be used as a shortcut key to access the group of controls rapidly.

✔ The attribute **align** positions the legend at the top (<LEGEND **align**=*top*>), the bottom (*bottom*), to the left (*left*) or to the right (*right*) of the group of controls.

....

<LABEL>...</LABEL>

Label a control of the form

> This element gives a label to the control of a form.

✔ The attribute **for** determines the related control.

✔ The attribute **accesskey** specifies a single character to be used as a shortcut key to focus the LABEL element concerned.

The LABEL element reacts to events; in addition to the standard event-driven attributes, it has the attributes **onfocus** and **onblur**.

4. Images

<IMG>

Insert an image

> This element is used to insert a GIF, JPG or PNG image in the document.

It's easy to place an image on the left, centre or right of the browser's window.

<P><IMG SRC="mit7.jpg" Align="left"></P>

<P><IMG SRC="mit7.jpg" Align="center"></P>

<P><IMG SRC="mit7.jpg" Align="right"></P>

Place the image with 1 pixel accuracy

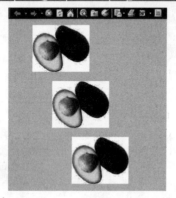

<IMG SRC="avocado.jpg" hspace=50>

<P><IMG SRC="avocado.jpg" hspace=100>

<P><IMG SRC="avocado.jpg" hspace=150>

 Try using 'vspace' to set vertical alignment.

✔ The attribute **src** specifies the URL of the image.

✔ The value of the attribute **alt** provides a text alternative if the browser cannot find the image or if the user does not want to display images; some browsers will display this value in a ToolTip whether the image is displayed or not.

✔ The attributes **width** and **height** fix the width and height of the image respectively, so you can, for instance, change the size of the image in the browser, or program a script that will enlarge the image if the mouse pointer passes over it.

IMG SRC="acamain.gif"

IMG SRC="acamain.gif" width=150 height=50

IMG SRC="acamain.gif" width=200 height=20

The main application of these attributes is that they enable the browser to reserve the space needed for the image and to continue to display the other objects, which can be downloaded faster, although modern browsers are fast enough to no longer need this feature.

✔ The attribute **border** determines the width (in pixels) of the border of the image. **Border**=*0* will make it impossible for the user to see any link.

IMG SRC="acamain.gif"

IMG SRC="acamain.gif" BORDER=10

Note

Clickable areas in an image

It is possible to define clickable areas on an image: to map the image.

✔ The attribute usemap of the IMG element gives the location of the image when the latter has clickable areas.

<IMG SRC= image1.gif USEMAP= #mapping >

The # means that the name of the map is a bookmark. The mapping is described in the MAP element in the same document.

. . . .

<MAP>...</MAP>

Map of an image with clickable areas

<MAP NAME=mapping>

Each clickable area is defined by an **AREA** element.

....
<AREA>

Area defined on an image in an MAP element

> <AREA SHAPE="CIRCLE" COORDS=
> "252,72,11" HREF="Hummer.htm">

✔ The attribute **shape** of the AREA element determines the nature of the area (*circle*, *rectangle* or *polygon*).

✔ The attribute **coords** of the AREA element gives the coordinates of the areas mapped on the image.

The following example simulates the display of "image1.gif", on which two clickable areas have been mapped (a complex polygon and a circle) by the AREA elements. Each area is linked to a URL.

✔ The browser will know that it must use this mapping when it encounters the attribute **usemap** of the IMG element.

```
<HTML><HEAD>

<TITLE>Clickable map</TITLE>

<BODY>

<IMG SRC="image1.gif" BORDER=0
USEMAP="#mapping">

<MAP NAME="mapping">

<AREA SHAPE="POLYGON"
COORDS="210,32,207,46,191,45,202,57,198,
69,214,62,226,71,224,56,235,49,214,45,206,3
2,207,32,210,32" HREF="Paddington.htm">

<AREA SHAPE="CIRCLE" COORDS=
"252,72,11" HREF="Hummer.htm">

</MAP></BODY></HTML>
```

Very many utilities can be used to draw clickable areas directly onto the image; the coordinates of the shapes will be measured automatically, and you can integrate them directly into the page under construction.

5. Particular elements

<DIV>...</DIV>
Independent container in the document

This element defines a generic block container. It is used with the CLASS element to define particular areas (e.g., a CLASS menu bar, or *navbar*) that are easy to edit on an entire site or to exclude from a printout.

Attribute: **align**=[*left* / *center* / *right* / *justify*] (horizontal alignment).

\<OBJECT\>...\</OBJECT\>
Universal container for objects

This element is a container to link most types of current objects to the document (images, videos, Java applets, VRML virtual worlds, etc.), but also types that have yet to be invented. In the long run, the **IMG** and **APPLET** elements will probably disappear and the **element** object will take over.

✔ The attribute **data** defines the URL of the target object.

✔ The attributes **width** and **height** define the dimensions of the object.

✔ The attribute **classid** specifies an implementation for the object, to comply with Java applets, Python applets, and ActiveX controls.

✔ The attribute **standby** provides text that will be displayed while the object is downloading.

The example that follows shows how alternative content can be presented if the user's browser does not have the necessary plug-in: first for a Python applet, then a Java applet, then a simple image, and finally a short text.

```
<OBJECT CLASSID="gyzmo.py"
codetype="application/x-python"
STANDBY="Ready to play Gyzmo?">

<OBJECT CLASSID="java:Gyzmo.class"
codetype ="application/java" WIDTH=400
HEIGHT=250 standby="Ready to see
Gyzmo?">

<OBJECT DATA="gyzmo.gif" type="image/
gif" width=200 height=100>The Gyzmo
Show.</OBJECT></OBJECT></OBJECT>
Note: 3<OBJECT> --> 3</OBJECT>
```

✔ The attribute **codetype** describes the medium needed for the implementation. These attributes save the browser from loading objects it is not equipped to run.

5

Tables

TABLES

Tables are often used to align different objects precisely on a page. With the new possibilities for the relative and absolute positions of objects, their use will undoubtedly decrease; but tables remain indispensable for organising the display of data.

Definition

A table is a grid of rows and columns that create cells. Rows can have different heights, and columns can have different widths.

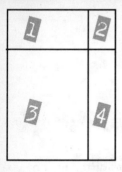

Table with 2 rows and 2 columns
that create 4 cells

A cell can extend over several rows
or several columns

Table with 2 rows and
2 columns. Cell 1 extends over
2 rows

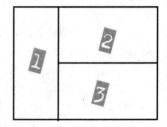

Table with 2 rows and
3 columns: cell 1 extends
over 2 columns, cell 2
extends over 2 rows

A cell can contain all types of objects: text, list, form, image or even another table. A cell can also be completely empty.

1. Table structure

A table is enclosed by the tags <TABLE> and </TABLE>.

Rows and columns

✔ The number of columns in the table is specified by the value (integer) of the optional attribute **cols**.

cols=*integer*

The code below defines a table with 2 columns:

```
<TABLE cols="2">
...the rest of the table...
</TABLE>
```

If the argument **cols** is not specified, the browser will have to wait for all the data in the table to finish downloading before deciding the number of columns and proceeding to display them. If the argument **cols** is specified, the displaying can begin as soon as the first data arrive.

The **TR** element is a container for the cells of a row defined in a table. The start tag **<TR>** is compulsory, the end tag **</TR>** is optional.

The following table contains three rows:

```
<TABLE>
<TR> ...A data row...
<TR> ...A second data row...
<TR> ...A third data row...
</TABLE>
```

Combining rows and columns

A table can combine rows and columns. The following code defines a table with two columns and three rows:

```
<TABLE cols="2">
<TR> ...First row...
<TR> ...Second row...
<TR> ...Third row...
</TABLE>
```

Table alignment, width, border and title

✔ The attribute **align** of the tag <TABLE> is used to position the table in relation to the document:

```
<TABLE align = left | center | right>
```

Value	Effect
left	The table is flush to the left margin.
center	The table is centred horizontally.
right	The table is flush to the right margin.

✔ The attribute **width** of the tag <TABLE> is used to define the width (horizontal dimension) of the table

<TABLE width=*length*>

If the attribute **width** is not specified, the width of the table will be determined by the browser.

The attribute **border** of the tag <TABLE> defines the width (in pixels) of the border round the table:

<TABLE border=*pixels*>

The attribute **frame** of the tag <TABLE> specifies the visibility of all or part of the frame of the table:

<TABLE frame= void | above | below | hsides | lhs | rhs | vsides | box | border>.

Value	Effect
void	No border is visible (default value).
above	Only the border above is visible.
below	Only the border below is visible.
hsides	The two horizontal sides are visible.
vsides	The two vertical sides are visible.
lhs	Only the left border is visible.
rhs	Only the right border is visible.
box	All four borders are visible.

The optional element **CAPTION** must be entered immediately after the start tag of the **TABLE** element:

```
<TABLE cols="4">
<CAPTION>Table caption </CAPTION>
...the rest of the table...
</TABLE>.
```

The start and end tags are compulsory.

✔ The attribute **align** is used to position the caption in relation to the table:

<CAPTION align = *top | bottom | left | right*>

Value	Effect
top	The caption is placed at the top of the table (default value).
bottom	The caption is placed at the bottom of the table.

left	The caption is placed to the left of the table.
right	The caption is placed to the right of the table.

```
<TABLE cols="4">

<CAPTION align=right>The caption is to the
right in relation to the table </CAPTION>
...the rest of the table...
</TABLE>
```

Groups of rows: the elements THEAD, TFOOT and TBODY

Groups of rows and of columns can be created in a table, and each group is given a header and a footer. This enables the browser to scroll the columns and rows of a large table while continuing to display the headers and footers.

A table must contain at least one group of rows. A group of rows is divided into three parts:

       1. header (THEAD element)

       2. footer (TFOOT element)

       3. body (TBODY element)

Each instance of the **THEAD**, **TFOOT**, and **TBODY** elements must contain at least one row (**TR**).

Example:

The code which follows shows the order of the different elements (THEAD, TFOOT and TBODY):

```
<TABLE>
<THEAD>
   <TR> ...header information...
</THEAD>
<TFOOT>
   <TR> ...footer information...
```

```
</TFOOT>
<TBODY>
  <TR> ...first row of first data block...
  <TR> ...second row of first data block...
</TBODY>
<TBODY>
  <TR> ...first line of second data block...
  <TR> ...second line of second data
block...
</TBODY>
</TABLE>
```

The declaration of the **TFOOT** element *must* appear before that of **TBODY** in a **TABLE** definition, so that the browser can display the table footer before it has received all the data (which can be sizeable) constituting the body of the row group.

If a table is body only (no header or footer) the tag <TBODY> can be omitted.

If a block of the table has a header, the tag <THEAD> is compulsory. The end tag </THEAD> can then be omitted if a start tag of **TFOOT** or **TBODY** element follows.

If a block of the table has a footer, the tag <TFOOT> is compulsory. The end tag </TFOOT> can then be omitted if a start tag of a **THEAD** or **TBODY** element follows.

The preceding example can therefore be coded as follows:

```
<TABLE>
<THEAD>
  <TR> ...header information...
<TFOOT>
  <TR> ...footer information...
<TBODY>
```

```
    <TR> ...first row of first data block...
    <TR> ...second row of first data block...
</TBODY>
<TBODY>
    <TR> ...first row of second data block...
    <TR> ...second row of second data
block...
</TBODY>
</TABLE>.
```

Groups of columns:
the COLGROUP element

A table must contain at least one column group. If no group of columns is explicitly defined, the browser will assume that all the columns of the table form an implicit group.

A group of columns in a table starts with the tag **<COLGROUP>**. The end tag **</COLGROUP>** is optional. The **COLGROUP** element explicitly creates a column group.

✔ The optional attribute **span** specifies the number (integer) of columns.

  Default value: *1*.
  The browser will ignore this attribute if the column group contains at least one COL element.

✔ The attribute **width** applied to the COLGROUP element specifies the default width for the columns.

  Width value =*length*.
  The special value *0** tells browsers to use for each column the minimum size necessary to display the content of the widest cell.

 If a COL element is present, the effect of this value could be disturbed.

The example which follows contains two column groups. The first group contains eight columns, the second contains six. The default width of the columns of the first group is 50 pixels. The width of the columns of the second group is the minimum width required to display the columns.

```
<TABLE>
<COLGROUP span="8" width="50">
<COLGROUP span="6" width="0*">
<THEAD>
<TR> ...
</TABLE>
```

The **COL** element is used to define the attributes for several columns in a column group and assign identical values to the columns. One or more **COL** elements can be included in each column group explicitly defined by the **COLGROUP** element.

Example:

The code which follows defines a table with visible rules (see bottom of page 163):

```
<FONT FACE="ARIAL" COLOR="#FFFFFF">

<TABLE BORDER=10 cellspacing=5
rules=cols>

<TD width=33% bgcolor=black>

<TD>

<IMG SRC="1032crouton.jpg">

<TD width=33% bgcolor=lightblue>

</TABLE>
```

A table with 3 columns. The central column contains a picture.

The rules are visible (attribute rules).

The start tag <COL> is compulsory.

The end tag (which would be </COL>) is prohibited.

✔ The attribute **width** defines the width of all the columns. It functions as for COLGROUP (see 4.2) to fix the width of the columns but can also take the value n^*, where n is an integer. It is then a relative width. In allocating the free space to rows and columns, the browser starts by reserving the space of elements defined in an absolute manner (so many pixels or such a percentage of space), then divides the space remaining between the rows or columns that remain. Each row or column defined in relative terms is allotted part of the space in proportion to the integer preceding the *. The value * is equivalent to 1*.

The table in the example that follows contains two column groups. The first group contains three columns, the second only two. The browser will reserve 30 pixels for the first column. The minimum space needed for the second column is calculated, then reserved. The remaining horizontal space in the table will be divided into six equal portions. Two of these portions are attributed to column three, three to column four, and finally one to column five.

Note

The optional attribute span of the COL element

If the attribute span is absent, each COL element represents one column.

If the attribute span is allotted a value n > 0, the element COL is equivalent to n columns of the table.

If the attribute span is given the value 0, the COL element is applied to all the remaining columns of the table, including the current one.

```
<TABLE>
<COLGROUP align="center">
 <COL width="30">
 <COL width="0*">
 <COL width="2*">
<COLGROUP >
 <COL width="3*" align="char" char=":">
 <COL width="1*">
<THEAD>
<TR> ...
</TABLE>
```

We have defined the attribute **align** of the first column group as *center*. All the cells of the three columns of this group will inherit this value (their content will be centred).

The penultimate COL element aligns the cells of the column on the character ':'.

The browser must interpret the code to display the number of rows and columns of the table correctly. For the rows, the task is simple: all it has to do is count the **<TR>** elements.

To count the columns, however, the browser can use different methods:

- ➡ it can examine each row to calculate the necessary number of columns (spanned as necessary);

- ➡ it can count the columns defined by the **COL** and **COLGROUP** elements.

The definition for the argument **col** of the tag **<TABLE>** seems to settle the problem once and for all. The following code:

> **<TABLE cols=4>**

> will be enough for the browser to draw four columns.

If the value of **cols** is greater than the result of the calculation above, the browser will end the row with the necessary number of empty cells.

Nevertheless, a browser may encounter problems when comparing its counts with the value stipulated by the argument **cols**, and it is best to use the **COL** and **COLGROUP** elements (which also make it possible to provide additional width data) for the properties of the columns.

2. Table cells: the elements TH and TD

When columns and rows are defined in a table, cells are created automatically. These cells can be empty. The first cell of a column or a row can receive particular data: the headers. It is worth making it possible for the browser to distinguish these header cells, so that they can be displayed on the screen at all times while scrolling through a long table, for instance.

The **TH** element specifies the header cell of a column or a row. The **TD** element specifies all other cells. The start tag is compulsory, the end tag is optional.

The following table contains five data columns, each with a header:

```
<TABLE border="border">

<CAPTION>Favourite aperitif
</CAPTION>

<TR> <TH>Name<TH>Type
<TH>Brand<TH>Otherwise<TH>Ice?

<TR> <TD> JP Lovinfosse<TD>Whisky
<TD>Old Dundee <TD>Scotch<TD>Yes

<TR> <TD>Aya Redone <TD>Water
<TD>Perrier <TD>Nothing <TD>No

</TABLE>.
```

The **border** attribute enables the browser to show the difference between headers and data more clearly.

Favourite aperitif

Name	Type	Brand	Otherwise	On the rocks ?
JP Lovinfosse	Whisky	Old Dundee	Scotch	Yes
Aya Redone	Water	Perrier	Nothing	No

Identifying Cells

Identifying a cell means making it correspond to a database field, so that transfers can take place between the document (at the client end) and the database (at the server end), or vice versa. Browsers capable of voice synthesis can also make extensive use of this identification to read (or write to) a given cell.

✔ The attributes **axis** and **axes** of the TD element give each cell a label (axis identifies the row, axes the column):

   axis = *data*
   Default value: the content of the cell
   axes = *list of data*

In the example below, the attribute **axis** takes the value of the family name, and the attribute **axes** takes the value of the column header.

```
<TABLE border="border">

<CAPTION>Favourite aperitif
</CAPTION>

<TR> <TH>Name <TH>Type <TH>Brand
<TH>Otherwise<TH>Ice?

<TR> <TD axis="Lovinfosse" axes=
"Names"> JP Lovinfosse<TD>Whisky
<TD>Old Dundee <TD>Scotch<TD>Yes

<TR> <TD axis="Redone" axes=
"Names">Aya Redone <TD>Water
<TD>Perrier <TD>Nothing <TD>No

</TABLE>
```

Spanning cells over several rows or columns

A cell can span more than one row and/or more than one column.

This spanning is defined by the attributes **rowspan** and **colspan** of the TD and TH elements.

· ·
rowspan=*integer*

Specifies the number of rows that the cell will span. Default value: *1*. The value *0* extends the cell to all the rows after the row of the cell considered.

· ·
colspan=*integer*

Specifies the number of columns that the cell will span. Default value *1*. The value *0* extends the cell to all the columns after the column of the cell considered.

✔ The Boolean attribute **nowrap** of the **TD** and **TH** elements obliges the browser to ignore the automatic wrap, which can cause inordinately large (and therefore illegible) cells. It is better to avoid using this attribute and to opt for the appropriate attribute of a style sheet.

Example:

In the table below, the cell of the third data row, second column, will span two columns.

```
<TABLE border="border">

<CAPTION>Spanning of a cell </CAPTION>

<TR> <TH>Column 1 <TH>Column 2
<TH>Column 3<TH>Column 4

<TR> <TD>1<TD>2<TD>3<TD>4

<TR> <TD>5<TD colspan="2"><TD>8

</TABLE>
```

Cell span			
Column 1	Column 2	Column 3	Column 4
1	2	3	4
5			8

Spanned cells cause a shift which may confuse certain browsers.

When cells spanned over several rows or columns are crossed, overlaid cells can be obtained, which provide an interesting field for entering text on an image, for example, as each of these objects is in a different cell.

In the following table, cell 4 spans two rows and cell 5 two columns. These two cells cover a common section.

Browsers' behaviour in such circumstances must be checked carefully.

```
<TABLE border="border">
<TR><TD>1 1 1... <TD>2 2 2...
<TR><TD>3 3 3... <TD rowspan="2">4 4 4...
<TR><TD colspan
="2">5 5 5 ...
</TABLE>
```

1 1 1...	2 2 2...
3 3 3...	4 4 4...
5 5 5...	

Aligning the content of cells

Horizontal alignment of the content and justification of the text in the cell is governed by:

align = *left* | *center* | *right* | *justify* | *char*

Value	Effect
left	Default value (TD). The cell is filled from the left. Text is aligned left.
center	Default value (TH). The cell is filled from the centre. Text is centred.
right	The cell is filled from the right. Text is aligned right.
justify	The text is justified left and right.
char	Text is justified by alignment on a given character.

ALIGN

Left	Right	Center	Default
1	2	3	4

Vertical alignment
of the content of a cell

This is governed by:

valign = *top | middle | bottom | baseline*

Value	Effect
top	The cell is filled from the top.
middle	Default value. The content is centred vertically.
bottom	The cell is filled from the bottom.
baseline	If the attribute **valign** takes this value in a cell, all the cells of the same row will be aligned on the same baseline.

Aligning text on a given character in a cell

char=*data*

Specifies a character that will be used as an aligning mark. By default, the alignment will be carried out on the decimal separator ('.'). NB: the value of the attribute is case-sensitive.

....

charoff=*length*

Not all the cells whose text has to be aligned to the character defined by **char** necessarily contain this character. In this case, the attribute **charoff** is taken into account. It fixes the indent (in pixels or percentage of the cell width) of the text in the cell if it does not contain the alignment character.

Alignment inheritance

The alignment of the content of a cell can be defined:

- in the cell itself;

- in an element that contains the cell (row, column); this is called inheritance, and the question arises as to the priorities between attributes fixed at different levels.

The priority (from highest to lowest) for defining the attributes **align**, **char**, and **charoff** is as follows:

1. inside the data of a cell (P, for example);
2. for a cell (TH or TD);
3. a column or group of columns (COL and COLGROUP);
4. a row or group of rows (TR, THEAD, TFOOT and TBODY);
5. the element (TABLE);
6. default alignment.

The priority (from the highest to the lowest) for **valign** (and the other inherited attributes **lang**, **dir** and **style**) is the same as above, except that priorities 3 and 4 are reversed. The default alignment cell depends on the browser.

3. Spacing between cells

The attributes **cellspacing** and **cellpadding** of the tag <TABLE> define the spacing between cells and their interior margin.

<TABLE cellspacing = length>

This attribute specifies the spacing between the frame of the table and the border of the cells at the edge of the table, as well as the cells inside the table.

Cellspacing=10

Left	Right	Center	Default
1	2	3	4

<TABLE cellpadding=length>

This attribute specifies the space between the interior border of a cell and its content, in all directions.

Cellpadding=10

| 1 | 2 | 3 | 4 |

Cellpadding=1

| 1 | 2 | 3 | 4 |

Example:

In the following table, the attribute **cellspacing** specifies a space of 10 pixels between the cells, and a space of 10 pixels between the edge cells and the table frame.

The attribute **cellpadding** specifies that the top margin and the bottom margin are each 25% of the total cell height (i.e., 50% of the empty vertical space for the two margins). Similarly, the left and right margin are 25% of the cell width (i.e., 50% of the empty horizontal space for the two margins).

```
<TABLE><TR cellspacing="10">
<TD>Data1 <TD cellpadding="50%">Data2
<TD>Data3</TABLE>
```

4. Gutters

✔ The attribute **rules** of the tag <TABLE> defines the gutters between cells.

```
<TABLE rules = none |
groups | rows | cols |
all>
```

Default

Data1 Data2 Data3
Data4 Data5 Data6

Rules=all

Data1	Data2	Data3
Data4	Data5	Data6

Rules=cols

Data1	Data2	Data3
Data4	Data5	Data6

Rules=rows

Data1 Data2 Data3
Data4 Data5 Data6

Value	Effect
none	No gutter (default value).
groups	Gutters appear between the rows groups (cf. THEAD, TFOOT and TBODY) and the column groups (cf. COLGROUP and COL).
rows	Horizontal gutters appear between the rows.
cols	Vertical gutters appear between the columns.
all	Gutters appear between all the cells.

Colour in tables

✔ The attribute **bgcolor** defines the background colour of the following tags:

<Body bgcolor=color>

   for an entire document

<Table bgcolor= color>

   for an entire table

<TR bgcolor= color>

   for a complete row

<TD bgcolor= color> or **<TH bgcolor= color>**

   for a cell

 This attribute became obsolete with HTML version 4. It should be replaced by the appropriate attributes in a style sheet.

Direction in tables: the attribute dir

A browser reads a table from left to right by default. The first column is therefore at the far left, and the first row is at the top. The opposite direction can also be defined (Right To Left):

```
<TABLE dir="RTL">
...the rest of the table...
</TABLE>.
```

The effects of this attribute are as follows:

- •• the first column is at the far right, but the first row is still at the top;

- •• any empty cells are added to the left;

- •• the cells inherit the attribute: the text will be entered from right to left; in fact, the blocks inherit the attributes, but as there is at least one block by default, the effect is passed on to the cells, even if there is no explicit group. The argument **dir** can be applied to correct the direction of the content: a table running from right to left is then obtained, but with cells with text running from left to right.

6

Frames: windowed documents

FRAMES: WINDOWED DOCUMENTS

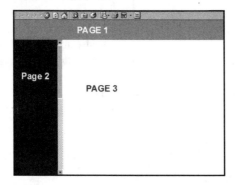

A document that contains three others.

A document written in HTML can contain other documents of the same type. This is known as *windowing*, where each document is contained in a *frame*. Numerous configurations are possible, from the simplest to the most complex, depending on the desired result.

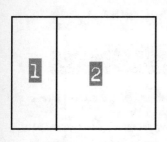

Here we have two frames. If we take the example of a magazine, frame 1 could contain a Web page used as a summary, while frame 2 would contain the Web page referred to in the summary. Frame 1 would thus serve as a 'table of contents', always displayed on the screen.

In this more complex structure:

frame 1 could be used to display permanent information (e-mail address, title of the magazine, etc.);

the summary is placed in frame 2;

the page chosen in the summary appears in frame 3;

frame 4 could be used for adverts.

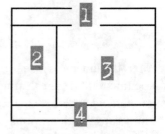

The structures can be very complex, as a frame can in turn contain other frames.

> ### Note
>
> **Each visible frame is an independent HTML document.**
>
> **The frames are located in another document, which serves as a container. To construct the example above, you need a container document plus five documents: one per frame.**

<FRAMESET>...</FRAMESET>
The container document for the frames

In the structure of an HTML document, the **FRAMESET** element replaces the BODY element.

This element is a container for the rectangular areas called *frames*.

A frame is contained in a **FRAME** element. Each frame contains an HTML document.

The **frameset** element can contain one or more **frame** elements and even one or more **frameset** elements, as well as a **noframes** element to display alternative content if the browser does not support windowing.

✔ The attributes **rows** and **cols** fix the dimensions of each frame, in pixels or in percentages of the available space.

The **frameset** element accepts the event-driven attributes **onload** and **onunload**.

....

<FRAME>

This element defines a rectangular frame in the FRAMESET element.

✔ The attribute **src** specifies the URL of the document that must be displayed in the element. In theory, any resource could be invoked (e.g., an image), but it is best to include this resource in the Web page.

✔ The attribute **name** gives the identifier of the frame. This attribute is compulsory, and its value must start with a character (A–Z, a–z). The identifier is essential because it will be used to determine the target frame of a link: for example, if you click a link in frame 1, you must specify (by means of the attribute target) the name of the frame in which the invoked document is to be displayed.

✔ The attribute **frameborder** determines whether the border of the frame will be visible (**frameborder**=*1*, default value) or invisible (**frameborder**=*0*).

✔ The attributes **marginwidth** and **marginheight** define (in pixels) the width and the height of the internal margins of the frame.

✔ The Boolean attribute **noresize** prevents the user resizing the frame.

✔ The attribute **scrolling** determines whether the frame can (**scrolling**=*yes*) or cannot (**scrolling**=*no*) have scrollbars, and whether the scrollbars will appear only if necessary (**scrolling**=*auto*, default value).

<NOFRAMES>...</NOFRAMES>
Alternative content to windowing

Some browsers do not support windowing, so you must provide an alternative display for them in the **NOFRAMES** element.

The NOFRAMES element must contain the **BODY** element.

Appendices

APPENDIX 1

Formal inline elements

A - ABBR - ACRONYM - B - BASEFONT - BDO - BIG - BR - CITE - CODE - DFN - EM - FONT - I - IMG - INPUT - KBD - LABEL - Q - S - SAMP - SELECT - SMALL - SPAN - STRIKE - STRONG - SUB - SUP - TEXTAREA - TT - U -VAR

Formal block elements

ADDRESS - BLOCKQUOTE - CENTER - DIR - DIV - DL - FIELDSET - FORM - H1 - H2 - H3 - H4 - H5 - H6 - HR - ISINDEX - MENU - NOFRAMES - NOSCRIPT - OL - P - PRE - TABLE - UL

Elements that can be considered block in the BODY element

DD - DT - FRAMESET - LI - TBODY - TD - TFOOT - TH - THEAD - TR

Elements that can be considered either block or inline (in the latter case, they may contain block elements)

APPLET - BUTTON - DEL - IFRAME - INS - MAP - OBJECT - SCRIPT

APPENDIX 2

Entities (complex characters)

Codes for the main complex characters

Character	Entity	Decimal	Hexadecimal
"	"	"	"
&	&	&	&
<	<	<	<
>	>	>	>
Œ	Œ	Œ	Œ
œ	œ	œ	œ
_	Š	Š	Š
_	š	š	š

ˆ	&circ;	&#710;	&#x2C6;
˜	&tilde;	&#732;	&#x2DC;
_			
–	&ndash;	&#8211;	&#x2013;
—	&mdash;	&#8212;	&#x2014;
'	&lsquo;	&#8216;	&#x2018;
'	&rsquo;	&#8217;	&#x2019;
‚	&sbquo;	&#8218;	&#x201A;
"	&ldquo;	&#8220;	&#x201C;
"	&rdquo;	&#8221;	&#x201D;
„	&bdquo;	&#8222;	&#x201E;
†	&dagger;	&#8224;	&#x2020;
‡	&Dagger;	&#8225;	&#x2021;
‰	&permil;	&#8240;	&#x2030;

Glossary

Glossary

ActiveX

ActiveX is a set of technologies from Microsoft that enables interactive content for the World Wide Web.

Anchor

In HTML, anchors mark the start and end of hypertext links.

Applet

A small program that can be embedded in an HTML page.

ASCII (American Standard Code for Information Interchange).

This is the de facto world-wide standard for the code numbers used by computers to represent all the upper- and lowercase Latin letters, numbers, punctuation, etc. There are 128 standard ASCII codes, each of which can be represented by a seven-digit binary number : 0000000 to 1111111.

Bookmark

A feature of most Web browsers. You can save frequently accessed links in a bookmark file, rather than having to look up the URL each time.

Browser

A client program that allows users to access various kinds of Internet resources.

Bullet

In HTML, a bullet is a dot used to separate listed items on a Web page

CGI (Common Gateway Interface)

A set of rules that describe how a Web server communicates with another piece of software on the same machine, and how the other piece of software (the 'CGI program' or 'CGI script') talks to the Web server. Any piece of software can be a CGI program if it handles input and output according to the CGI standard.

Cgi-bin

The most common name of a directory on a Web server in which CGI programs are stored.

Checkbox

In HTML, a way to allow the user to interact with the material on a Web page by clicking on a box or other input element.

Clickable image map

An image where certain parts of it are associated with different hyperlinks.

Client

1 A software program that is used to contact and obtain data from a server software program on another distant computer. Each client program is designed to work with one or more specific kinds of server programs, and each server requires a specific kind of client (a Web Browser).

2 A remote computer connected to a host or server computer.

Cookie

The most common meaning of 'cookie' on the Internet refers to a piece of information sent by a Web server to a Web browser that the browser software is expected to save and to send back to the server whenever the browser makes additional requests from the server. Cookies might contain information such as login or registration information, online 'shopping card' information, user preferences, etc.

Domain name

The address that identifies an Internet site. Domain names consist of at least two parts. The part on the left is the name of the company, institution or other organization. The part on the right identifies the highest subdomain. This can be a country, such as ca for Canada, fr for France, or the type of organization: com for commercial, edu for educational, etc. The IP address is translated into the domain name by the DNS.

DNS (Domain Name System)

A database system that translates an IP address into a domain name. For example, a numeric address like 105.204.103.10 is converted into wwraw.com.

Download

To transfer files from one computer to another. The most common way of doing this on the Internet is by FTP.

DTD (Document Type Definition)

This is the formal specification of a markup language, written using SGML (an ISO set of specifications). HTML has a DTD.

E-mail (electronic mail)
A way of sending messages between computers attached to local or global networks.

Embedded hyperlink
A hyperlink that is incorporated into a line of text.

Feedback form
Sections of HTML documents that accept user input for comments, to order products, or to search for information.

Font
Complete set of printed or display characters of the same typeface, size and style.

Form
Forms are used to accept user information into a browser page and then pass that data to a script or process (usually CGI scripts) to be run by the Web server host machine.

Form support
Not all browsers, nor all servers, can handle the use of forms where the reader can give input, for instance a question.

FTP (File Transfer Protocol)

A way of moving files across networks. With FTP you can login to another Internet site and download or send files.

CGI script

Common Gateway Interface program (typically written by Web authors for the sole purpose of processing their form data) located on a Web server that processes information entered on a form and provides a response of some sort.

GIF (Graphic Interchange Format)

A common format for image files, especially suitable for images containing large areas of the same colour.

Home page (or Homepage)

1 The Web page that your browser is set to display automatically when it starts up.

2 The first page on a Web site that acts as the starting point for navigation.

Host

1 Any computer on a network that is a repository for services available to other computers on the network.

2 A computer that acts as a server.

Hotspot

A place in a document that contains an embedded hyperlink.

HTML (Hypertext Markup Language)

The coding language used to create hypertext documents (HTML files) for use on the World Wide Web. Files in HTML format are viewed with a World Wide Web client program (browser).

HTTP (Hypertext Transfer Protocol)

The protocol for moving hypertext files across the Internet. It requires an HTTP client program (browser) on one end, and an HTTP server program on the other end. HTTP is the most important protocol used on the World Wide Web.

Hyperlinks

These are links in HTML documents that you can click on to go to other Web resources.

Hypermedia

The multimedia links on the Web that lead to sound, graphics, video or text resources.

Hypertext

Hypertext is the basic organizing principle of the WWW. Generally, it is any text that contains hyperlinks.

Inline image

A built-in graphic that is displayed by the browser as part of an HTML document.

Integer

Any whole number. Integers may be positive or negative. Zero is an integer, and is often considered positive.

Internet account

An account with an ISP that allows you to access the Internet

Interpretation engine

Part of a browser that translates and executes the code written in a high-level language like HTML.

Intranet

A private network inside a company or organization that uses the same kinds of software that you would find on the Internet, but that is only for internal use.

IP address

The Internet Protocol address – the numeric address that is translated into a domain name by the DNS.

IP number (Internet Protocol number)

A unique number consisting of four parts separated by dots, e.g. 205.165.127.4. Every machine on the Internet has a unique IP number – if a machine does not have an IP number, it is not really on the Internet. Most machines also have one or more domain names that are easier for people to remember.

ISP (Internet Service Provider)

An institution or a company that provides access to the Internet in some form, usually for money.

Java

Java is a network-oriented programming language invented by Sun Microsystems that is specifically designed for writing programs that can be safely downloaded to your computer through the Internet and immediately run without fear of viruses or other harm to your computer or files. Using small Java programs (called 'applets'), Web pages can include functions such as animations, calculators, and other fancy tricks.

JPG, JPE, JPEG (Joint Photographic Experts Group)

JPEG is most commonly mentioned as a format for image files. JPEG format is preferred to the GIF format for photographic images as opposed to line art or simple logo art.

Keyword

A word or phrase that is intended to aid the end user in finding help on a particular topic or topics. Each topic may have one or more keywords assigned to it.

Link (hyperlink)

Links are used to move from one location to another: to a new page, or to an entry within the current page, or to an entry point within another page.

Load

On the Web, HTML documents and graphics are loaded into the browser whenever an URL is accessed.

Local script

A program written in JavaScript or VBScript and embedded in the HTML document.

Metadata

Meta tags are used in the HEAD section of a page. They store information such as author, keywords, etc. and may be used for indexing or searching.

Navigate

To move around on the Web by following hypertext paths from document to document on different computers.

Netiquette

The rules of etiquette that guide online interaction on the Internet.

Online

When a user is connected to a network, they are described as being online.

Password

A code used to gain access to a locked system. A secret combination of letters and other symbols needed to login to a computer system.

Pixel (picture element)

Pixels are the small dots that make up the image on your computer screen. Currently, most PC monitors are set at a pixel resolution of 800 by 600, which means that the image across the entire screen is 800 pixels wide and 600 pixels high.

Plug-in

A small piece of software that adds features to a larger piece of software. The idea behind plug-ins is that a small piece of software is loaded into memory by the larger program, adding a new feature, and that users need only install the few plug-ins that they need, out of a much larger pool of possibilities.

PNG (Portable Network Graphics)

An image format available on the Internet (like GIF and JPEG images).

Protocol

A specification that describes how computers communicate with each other on a network.

Python applet

An applet written in Python, an interpreted, interactive, object-oriented, extensible programming language.

Radio button
Used in forms to indicate a list of items. Only one button can be selected at one time.

Resource
Any file accessible on the Internet.

Search engine
Programs on the Internet that allow users to search through massive databases of information.

Server
A computer on a network that provides a specific kind of service to client software running on other computers. The term 'server' is also used to refer to a piece of software that makes the process of serving information possible.

Servlet
An applet running on a server. A CGI script is a servlet.

Surf
To search for information on the Web by navigating in a non-linear way.

Tags

Tags are the codes used to format HTML documents for the Web. There are single and compound tags. For example, the single code for a line break is <br>, whereas for bold text there are compound tags that require both an initial and a closing code: <b> </b>

Telnet

The command and program used to log in from one Internet site to another. The telnet command/program takes you to the login prompt of another host.

Text only format

Text saved in pure ASCII.

ToolTip Text

An alternative text message appearing while the mouse runs over an object.

Under construction

A term used to describe a Web site that is still being developed. A small graphic is often displayed instead of the pages or parts still being created or modified.

Unicode

Unicode provides a unique number for every character, no matter what the platform, no matter what the program, no matter what the language. Fundamentally, computers just deal with numbers. They store letters and other characters by assigning a number for each one. Before Unicode was invented, there were hundreds of different encoding systems for assigning these numbers. No single encoding could contain enough characters: for example, the European Union alone requires several different encodings to cover all its languages. Even for a single language like English, no single encoding is adequate for all the letters, punctuation, and technical symbols in common use.

URL (Uniform Resource Locator)

An address you use to tell your browser where to find a particular Internet resource. A URL looks like this:

http://wwli.com

or telnet://well.sf.ca.us

VBScript

A script language for embedded applets, based on Microsoft's Visual Basic.

WWW (World Wide Web)

1   The whole constellation of resources that can be accessed using Gopher, FTP, HTTP, Telnet, USENET, WAIS and some other tools.

2   The universe of hypertext servers (HTTP servers), which are the computers that allow text, graphics, sound files, etc. to be mixed together in a hypermedia-based system.

Index

Index